Artist's Studio

Painting

by Jenny Fretland VanVoorst

Bullfrog
Books

Ideas for Parents and Teachers

Bullfrog Books let children practice reading informational text at the earliest reading levels. Repetition, familiar words, and photo labels support early readers.

Before Reading

- Discuss the cover photo. What does it tell them?
- Look at the picture glossary together. Read and discuss the words.

Read the Book

- "Walk" through the book and look at the photos. Let the child ask questions. Point out the photo labels.
- Read the book to the child, or have him or her read independently.

After Reading

- Prompt the child to think more. Ask: What sorts of things do you like to paint? Have you ever painted something you were especially proud of?

Bullfrog Books are published by Jump!
5357 Penn Avenue South
Minneapolis, MN 55419
www.jumplibrary.com

Library of Congress Cataloging-in-Publication Data

Fretland VanVoorst, Jenny, 1972–
   Painting / by Jenny Fretland VanVoorst.
      pages cm. — (Artist's studio)
   Includes index.
   ISBN 978-1-62031-282-7 (hardcover: alk. paper) —
   ISBN 978-1-62496-342-1 (ebook)
   1. Painting—Juvenile literature. I. Title.
ND1146.F74 2015
750—dc23
                                        2015021763

Series Designer: Ellen Huber
Book Designer: Michelle Sonnek
Photo Researcher: Michelle Sonnek

Photo Credits: All photos by Shutterstock except: 123RF, 10–11; CanStock, 6–7; Corbis, 10–11; Dreamstime, 8, 24; Glow Images, 5; iStock, 9; SuperStock, 4, 12–13, 20–21; Thinkstock, 3, 18–19, 22tr.

Printed in the United States of America at Corporate Graphics in North Mankato, Minnesota.

Table of Contents

Painter's Studio

Sal is a painter.

He works in a studio.

Sal paints abstract scenes.
He uses oil paints.

Sal paints on a canvas.

He uses bold colors.

He makes thick strokes with his brush.

9

All done. Look!

Do you like
Sal's painting?

Lea is a painter, too.
She paints outside.

Lea sets up her easel.

She takes out her watercolors.

She will paint the forest.

Lea adds water
to the paint.

Water makes
the colors flow.

All done. Look!

Do you like
  Lea's painting?

19

Try it yourself!
Painting is fun.

A Painter's Tools

brushes

palette

canvas

paints

Picture Glossary

abstract
A painting style that makes little or no attempt at creating a realistic picture.

oil paints
A paint whose liquid part is oil.

canvas
A piece of cloth used as a surface for painting.

studio
The working place of an artist.

easel
A frame for supporting an artist's canvas.

watercolors
A paint whose liquid part is water.

Index

To Learn More

Learning more is as easy as 1, 2, 3.

1) Go to www.factsurfer.com

2) Enter "painting" into the search box.

3) Click the "Surf" button to see a list of websites.

With factsurfer.com, finding more information is just a click away.